BELLS FOR HER

Samantha Ledger

NeoPoiesis Press, LLC

NeoPoiesis Press
P.O. Box 38037
Houston, Texas 77238-8037

www.neopoiesispress.com

Copyright © 2010 by Samantha Ledger

All rights reserved. No part of this book may be used or reproduced in any manner whatsoever without express written permission from the publisher except in the case of brief quotations embodied in critical articles and reviews.

Bells for Her by Samantha Ledger
ISBN10 0-981-99845-3 (paperback : alk. paper)
   1. Poetry. I. Ledger, Samantha

Printed in the United States of America.

First Edition

Also by Samantha Ledger:

Everybody Else's Girl
Copyright 2007, by d/e/a/d/b/e/a/t/ Publishing
ISBN 978-0-6151-7662-8 (paper: alk. paper)

For Vega & Lyra
Forever you shall be amongst the stars

Contents

Mourning's Playtime

the weed 2
like bleeding; like love 3
midnight blue 6
loves simple sickness 7
tie me to the oak tree 8
woolgatherings 10
mourning's playtime 11
little bird 12
Christmas 1994 14
malfeasance's fable 16
birth 18

Sins and Sinners

breakfast at the corner cafe 20
Jackie says I should tell him no 23
drinking whiskey from a dirty glass 24
aborting mother 26
the market by the arches 28
London 30
concave 31
November's child 34
Wednesday's child 36
laggard 37
I am a Death watch song 38
paper mâché darling 39
an ugly night in Soho 40

the game 42
the dark water nymph 44
the God squad 45
night watch Death song 46
quiet house 48

The Effigy of Self and Survival

Phoenix sunrise 50
girl loves girl loves girl 53
secret love notes 54
a love so strong 56
falseness of truth 58
moon 59
the feminine violation 60
letter 2003 61
for you 64
if I could be 66
reflective distortion 68
when I lay down in your bed of ashes 72
horripilation 74
woman of shadows 76
down by the water 78
foreign friend 80
there is nothing better than sex in the kitchen 82
ashes to ashes 84
if the wings of Icarus had been made of steel 86
Death turns clever in my mind 87
re crim in ation 88
otiose 90
incandescence 91
to an end 92

Pulling Wings from Dragonflies

the fingersmith 94
genetic disorder 96
embryonic ghost 98
blind death 99
sexual disqualification 100
how long must this last 102
my virtuoso villain 104
electra 106
circumlocution 108
of love I spoke 110

Mourning's Playtime

the weed

i am the shame.
the sex of men lingers in my belly,
churning into the meaning of myself,
their seed sown
swallowed down, with a hungered longing

I am the denial.
crippled, with the poison of their parts
stunned- stunted from further growth,
starved of air,
choking - on parts and limbs and life

I am the measurement.
five inches, for five years plus one
a cavernous youth, hollowed,
dug clean by constant ploughing,
their presence- full grown manhood

I am the lie.
choking on my own shame,
no longer do they come,
begging bowl and balls in clasped hand,
womanhood, a curvaceous deterrent

i am the delinquent.
the dandelion girl,
unfurling petals, a ravenous weed

when i go to seed, i shall sow myself
far and wide - at the mercy of the winds,
these parts, scattering becoming lost
echoing memories of themselves

like bleeding; like love

Divine countenance,

counts for so little
when flesh has melded
to the cross

embedded

in my chest;
silent prayers mumbled
beneath sheet of crisp linen.

Supper time and you said

*Bow your head and read me
lines from King James;*

flames, fire and brimstone,

how my lack of
gratitude
slaps fast at your

face.

There is no grace
in my movements.

Fits of purposeless

agony

gripping hard small muscles;
much forgotten...
unused until now.

And how you sneer
where tears

blister in my eyes.

Deeper love
bleeds
like wounds.

Stigmata,

crucified upon your cross
of burgeoning manhood,
where I kneel
to give thanks
for supple inflexions
of your deep
throated voice.

I cannot rejoice

nor scream
or shout my disgust,
stifled under here
there is no room for

air

nor light of day;
only night's blackness;
a shroud of
un-deathliness.

When time becomes still,
in the measured run
of insides to the
outside,

I sop up your
remains
from weak legs,
pretend not to notice
the loss of myself

in the fluid mix.

I cannot fix you
nor I redeem myself.

This pained religion
darkly confined to
cornered rooms

is my love:
a letting of blood

for sins I cannot
understand

nor name.

midnight blue

Under my midnight blue
crinoline dress
lurks disturbed flesh,
stripped clean
by your fumbling finger
followed by its eager friend,
a fiend
scavenging for solace
in a virgin's bed.

Remains of innocence
pool warm at my bare feet,
such beauty
in ugly rivers
that run free
against nature's intent.
The indent of lust
pushes firm
but that is you.

A groove
or rhythm
it is singing off key
and it is screaming silent
inside this pretty head.
I am red raw
to your blackened statue.

Frozen and fearful,
I wait
for that horrendous hum-
the breathless drum of your
careless satisfaction.

loves simple sickness

calamities form, freed from confines
elicits a harrowed gaze -
on swirling flesh that buckles
with your engaging touch,

mottled with a weary breath;
sweat breaks the silence
with its pounding drip
to taint this white with filth;

above the waves lingers
your fresh kisses,
blackened tongue silencing
my own full mouthed scream,

I dream of waking fresh;
cleansed by haloed demons
who spoke with secret words,
anointing my head with holy water,

folded back into your soul
I nestle belligerent remains,
the darkened child of love's sickness
made in my mother's image,

such icons you worship
on bended knee,
to reach lowered heights
that small children demand,

back then your parched lips
crept over newly formed limbs,
fingers twisting in broken skin
and bones to a cracking delight,
here I rest with a burning disease;
seeping slow with fever
your insertion into here
leaves me hollowed.

tie me to the oak tree

let me run free,
roam wild in the grasses
that cover my scuffed knees,
too many years
have been spent
crawling on all fours -
waiting for forgiveness,

as sunshine warms me -
chilled bones fuse;
I become stiff and lifeless,
undone to the wind
that rushes through my hair,
knots of dirty love
snared in golden tresses,

when they come;
men lined one
after another,
I lay silent on the ground -
ready to give myself away,
never the bride -
no bouquets of roses
for this retch,

mother made me wash
in the cold stream
at the foot of garden,
to cleanse my pores
of the stench of sex,
yet no scrubbing could remove
the stain ingrained
upon my mind,

red ribbons billow in the breeze -
their freedom limited,
tied to branches
of the dead oak tree,

let them tie me to her
so crows may come
and peck out my eyes,
then I shall be free from seeing
mocking smiles
and curling fingers filled with lust.

woolgatherings

As daylight fades to the drifting horizon
there hangs off the crest of breaking waves
a delicate rocking of tides lulling eyes to heaviness.
When broken days fractured and sullen
gathered in small hands that search attentively for truth
we turn our eyes to the last blaze of sunlight
so we may blind our hearts from knowing.

Small voices call out across the land
to where they mingle with salt air,
washed out with wrecks caging the remains of lost men;
sailors from yesterday who sought freedom and adventure.
These youthful words seeking glory lay wasted
at the bottom among silt and seaweed,
forgotten when these children become full grown.

How each day merges with the last
into a dusty cloud of forgetfulness,
dreams laid bare in youth now stripped down,
bony remains bleached by the sun
until pure white we bury them in the sodden earth.

Last night daughters and sons knelt down
pressing small fingers tight into one another,
whispering prayers towards the starry skies.

Here laid in wait gilded angels
stretching their empty palms,
gathering together tender cares to hold
against their hearts ,
the warmth of love
before it turned to burnt ash and stone.

mourning's playtime

at the back of the school
where the church's grave yard
meets the woods
small children gather,
searching the remains
of strewn wreaths,
flowers as rotten
as the corpses
that lay underneath

the tender hands,
the weeping faces
that placed them
delicately on graves
of withered old women
and bitter old men
have returned
to their lives

now as playtime begins
the scavengers swarm,
picking at rain soaked ribbon
to decorate their camps
hidden between tress,
where many happy hours
pass between morning
and afternoon

in the summer
when the sun
beats through branches
a breeze lifting the summer dresses
of little girls

the ribbons of the dead
catch the light,
dancing to the tune
of youth's forgetful mourning

little bird

You run little bird;
for broken wings
cannot carry you
high into the air
where currents linger
to lift you
above the disarray.

*Who wounded you
little bird?*

Running along
a dirt track
that leads
to a menagerie
of trouble,

the cat is sitting
waiting for you,
but you can't see her
with your beady
black eye,
the other missing
when they poked you
with a sharp stick.

Soon your feathers
will scatter high;
settling on pavements
and tarmac roads,
where cars will weld
you bony remains
into an unforgiving ground.

No sound of mourning
will be heard
little bird,

the others
are silent
in their fear,
for no one knows
who broke your wings
and you cannot sing
out their name.

Christmas 1994

Poor whore baby with festering sores;
caught beneath the dress
borrowed from the best dressed ladyboy,
stands all coy in the neon light
blinking under the Tesco sign.

Mummy works the nine to five
bringing home the bacon,
two fat punters holding hands
behind her crocked back;
crack cooking over the scented Christmas candles.

And how the sandaled man comes ready
with open hands and book

preaching to Mrs. Dennis
on virtues of the holy life;
a wife to the Lord
and mother to her children.

How thin smeared red lips tremble
desire burning in blinded eyes;
cataracts cloudy white spreads
as infection rattles your iron lungs.

Redemption is a fickle fiction;
arrives too late wrapped with black ribbon.
The social turn up looking grave,
which they dug

27th December 1994
Four foot coffin lowered into the ground.

Found her busted up and broken
with the rotten veg and frozen turkey,.
two black eyes blistered from crying
trying to run from God's fearful gaze,
razor wire snagging her age 12 knickers.

Television screens filled with policemen
soon after the Queens speech at three.
We were having tea; sandwiches and Christmas cake.
The fake smiles plastered to a full fat face
and I moaned all the while the read out her name.

How ashamed to say I couldn't care less
that some undressed kid my age lay dead;
red from the cold and neglect.
Bored with my presents, I want T.V.
not she, but the hour long episode of Eastenders.

malfeasance's fable

You rest up on the esker.

Out of breath from climbing
I didn't comprehend that you had run
full pelt without stopping for a moment
just to see me here screaming.
Teaming with anger and misery,
singsong combinations of pain
scattered across my face,
the pace of your wheezing going ignored.

Back in the valley waits a gathering mob,
slobs and half breeds whose seeds intermingle.

Our family.

If you counted out fingers and toes
you would draw an uneven number.
Inbreeds that can't tie shoe laces or button up shirts,
except your father who wields a belt as if he was born with it
wrapped tight in his overgrown misshapen hand.
He was farmed on the land,
treats his women with less respect than his cattle all boney and
starved.

Sun long gone
dipped low behind the ridge,
stamping out the day with a steel-capped boot
muting light and warmth from our bones.

There is no home for us to run back to anymore.

We amble to the copse where the deer often stalk.
Slow…
For they may linger in shadows
deeper that the voice of the vicar
booming out his leaden sermon on a Sunday.

If I curl in your arms shall I sleep.

Deep into the dark until waking I shall know
that dreaming of things beyond our reach
only brings more tears that cannot wash away the dirt.

Skirt from this to that,
half in
half out,
as you gather sticks to fend off the beasts.
No fire
for they shall see the flames,
smell smoke from our burning shame.

Coming on horses
swooping into brambles with a searing rage
to grab hard the limbs of
small children,
we have become bound with words and fist to their saddles.

Back we shall go to the grind
and the dust
to rust into women that know nothing more.
Least we would be broken in two
and you and I
would be nothing more than fable.

birth

I wrap you in swaddling
your cold breath
chills my bare breast
draining me of my spirit,
the wanton child
clinging for dear life

a parasitic being
gnawing keenly of flesh,
anemic skin
turning yellow under lamps
of burning white,
examining parts damaged
by your violent arrival

stitched back with twine
a broken vessel,
clotting sheets drawn tight
to cure the indifference
that seeps in steady streams
from where you came
a screaming bundle of fury

Sins and Sinners

breakfast at the corner cafe

Fried English Breakfast
at the Corner Cafe'
the best way
to start a day after
waking drunk
from the night before.

So you say.

Your face is ragged
in the morning light;
streaming
from an open window,
yet the chilled air
does not stifle
the stench of your skin.

The grease from two
fat dick sausages
congeals with sauce
from half a tin
of baked beans.

Blood like plasma.

Are you envious of the proportion?
Do you know I am comparing you?

My head aches;
dull thumping
 remembering
the fucking of a
forgotten evening.

Swimming in the cost
of waking here with you.

Now I see...

through smoky haze
what you meant
when you said

You're a selfish lover.

I used you to forget;

to return to where I was
ten years back.
Add another nine
and we're at the beginning;
brimming with sick
unhinged men with
giant hands.

I slid into your bed,
into a groove of emotion
unknown to this self;
driven by the silent
child.

It was not me
that sucked your dick,
or rode hard
until you cried aloud;
proud at your manhood
as it drove her to
blackness;

it was she
who made me do that thing;

her two legs
wrapped tight around
your chest:

it was she
that tucked herself
into the crook of your arm

so harm
could be undone.

And now I know:
I fucked you to remember;

and shame
prickles my face
as I waste
four rashers,
beans,
sausages and
fried eggs.

Your crooked smile
of satisfaction turns me
inside myself.
How can you know and
how can I say?

You shagged a child
dressed as a woman

who fucked like a woman
because it's all
she's ever known.

Jackie says I should tell him no

Jackie says I should tell him "no."
when he comes knocking
full of drink and spite.
A fistful of love
stuffed hard in his trouser pocket,
a rocket grenade of lust
that pushes hard against my cheek.

She doesn't understand
I need his black fingernails
to run ragged through my hair,
or to feel his weight
and Bourbon breath upon my skin
in places that no other
would care to tread,
for I am dead beneath my nakedness.

Jackie says I should tell him "no."
not suck or blow him to sentimental gratitude.
She says with hidden jealousy,
that I am just his whore;
a mistress bent over or under
his heavy thumb
while his wife sits at home
full to bursting with his third child.

He says she doesn't understand him
or care for his sloppy touch;
fumbled grasps for satisfaction
in the dark and lonely night,
so I delight his little man

for I know in my own drunken stupor,
that I can only be real
as a meal served up when the fancy takes him
while his wife waits patiently cooking his dinner.

drinking whiskey from a dirty glass

I know why I drink.

Slumber like forgetfulness
entices me with
open arms.

Warm amber
tumbling over ice,
as cool or cold
as this broken heart.

A desire
driven from destruction
and hatefulness
of a selfish whore.
I am undone with my knowing,
so glow instead
with the red faced glaze
of a practised alcoholic.

Too often now I wake
exhausted.
Spent from a night
of swirling rooms
and sickness,
in the heavy arms
of a stranger.

Stagnant air
scented
with bodies and hard sex,
clothes strewn far and wide.

If I had died
happiness would sit here
smiling.
Instead shame runs rampant.

Running
with a drunk's stumble,
fumbling with buttons
down a street
whose name I do not know.
Searching
for some sense
in a thick-headed,
hung over state.

Home.

Rooms filled with empties,
cheese and something green
sitting in mouldy fridge.
No food to settle
a red raw stomach.
For there is too much
remembering
inside these walls.

My public house,
with thread bare carpets
and glass eyed barmaid,
will repair any
damage.

So I sit
to concede defeat,
drinking whisky
from a dirty glass.

Drinking myself back
to where forgetfulness
becomes an escape
from solitude's lonely
reflection.

aborting mother

Dearest Mother,
are you dead yet?
Or does regret
still hold firm
your black
broken heart.

Last week
your meek voice declared
through broken static
of your impending doom,
a gloom lingering
in the dull sound
of your easy vowels.

You never did
manage to mask
the cheap sound
of a lousy upbringing,
days spent
searching for coins
in gutters.

How you rushed;
boasted
about the gush
of the umber flow,
stemming from some
unseen wound;
a pain
gaining momentum
with each spasm.

Are you still drawing breath
or has death found its way
into the daylight?
Having crept
from the back alley

abortionist
who removed the growth
so many years ago.

A stinging irony
must now burn
in your soon to be removed
womb,
for there now is room
to grow tumours,
by your own
selfish
design.

How humorous
to watch your belly
getting fat,
filled with bile,
all the while you
fret about your looks
receding as a setting sun.
Or son?

Mummy, are you
as dead
as my sibling
laying rotten and forgotten
in some steel dish?
Do you wish
you had relented
to maternal instinct?

Or remain, or refrain
from thinking
too deeply,
but meekly
of neither right nor wrong,
but fondly
on the life you pretended
to live.

the market by the arches

In the half light
a crowd of
menacing youths hangs;

a dusk of malice and cheap cider.

The last of the vendors
fuelled with anger of a poor day's trade
eyeball us; suspicious.

You want a piece of these?

squeals a voice from the front of our gaggle,
squeezing teenage breasts

hard

an offering of
sympathy and self

hatred,

young white flesh trapped in a vice -
I realise as they stare it is me
calling out, selling my wares.

Jeers from within the group
circulate the men,

10 feet off...
they shake their greying heads...
a look of despair and desire
creasing their furrowed brows.

How they long to
plough away
at me
in the back alleys

where the soiled fruit gets

thrown.

The smudge of my red lips
curls to a sneer

Like you can even get it up.

My mouth runs away with itself again;
I fall short in shock
at my own filthy mind;

the bind of vodka and weed

a seed that sows deep
the need to burn skin with cigarettes.

When night has become
its own grown
menace, and men with
clear intent lurk
in long shadows smelling of

sweat,

I walk proud and
alone; home
where they
forget
my name,

through the
back alleys of
the market by the arches
praying
that someone will bite
as I dangle my hook;
I, the impaled
worm.

London

London town holds me tight in her fast grip -
the filth that swims around cold tethered feet,
lies that spill from an old whore's swaying hip
standing all night in red light's staving sleep,

men pushing on though the rush hour rain;
where she waits dreaming of feeding her kid,
his mind full of need to forget the pain -
her thoughts of sucking off the highest bid

down in the east end where the junkies go -
looking to score some high or sweet relief,
cooking up brown powder passes so slow
forgetting their mother consumed with grief,

the stories that weave though old London town -
streets paved with white gold until you fall down.

concave

when these eyes bleed
tears of joy - simple
in the efforts,
quiet lips shall lap
resplendent for love
at the feet
of men;
who bore me salvation
from the self,

can I contain these
urges?
locked deep
where you left
picture remains of yourself,
so I may witness
my own undoing
when the sun
sinks beneath the horizon,

contaminated lies;
how they run free
from me to the world,
does disgust sit
easily for you;
when you speak
of my betterment
under your wing
of imaginative learning,

mother would be so proud
if she could see
my new contortions,
twisted with attentive greed,
for your nod or grunts
of pleasurable approval
before showing me
all your worth,

when you broke me,
did knowing my size
please your pride?
often when I bind myself
to remembering
I smile with loss,
for all I am has fallen
to the floor,
I am as unclean now
as you

last night;
when I awoke alone
the grief
overwhelmed me,
for I had forgotten;
how much you hurt
when you invade me,

this lifeless whole
formed of flesh and blood
bleeds too often,
so my fertile dreams
are left unspoken,
so many men
have come to these waters;
yet none can measure
the simple delight
of fright you gave,

I am a concave girl;
strung of bone and twine,
left to dry out
in the burning
summer sun,
one day
perhaps you shall
return me to a form true,
and we shall
commune heavenly again,

the sin and sinner -
which am I?

November's child

They said you were born an a cold November day
when the night drew in early
enveloping the waning rays of sunlight
into the forming mist of a winters night.
Your small form squirming with fluids
as you emerged from the passage
of your mothers warmth,
father coiled tight against her breast
in absent minded observation - bated breath.

The first cries that rung from your wet lungs
hollow as the heart from which love bore you,
grasping fingers so small they were lost
in the swaddling wrap the nurses brought,
as you locked a tiny toothless mouth
into an iron grip around the burning nipple
of your young mothers heaving chest,
a swale of relief petered through the room.

Daddy paraded as a cock up and down
calling out in whoops of joy at your arrival,
the disaffected genes of two imbeciles
combining to create a small and glorious perfection.
Forgotten the remains of your fellows
buried one year before in the fallow ground,
a small coffin all in white
marking the purity of where he laid.

Cards and gifts began mounting
from the moment the news spread as wild fire,
relatives creeping from dark corners to rejoice
long live the carrier of the family name,
precious little bundle from passions fury you came
another fuck that faltered into procreation,
happy now the hearts that beat together
the kin of despair now standing in the wake of their saviour.

my own head buried beneath the covers
of my sick bed where I fermented my own contagions rage,
shamed that sibling rivalry has traversed a generation
to where my brothers child fresh into the world
caused a heart ache so strong I became paralysed.
Could this womb not succumb to positive longing
a seed unsown to linger long enough to hold
the lining of my being into fertilities delight.

Mother is not a word that is heard often here
aunt so tawdry when you wrestle with the truth
that brothers babies are those that should be yours,
many years spent beneath his growing manhood
his misspent adolescence forgotten - only my concern.
Holding back the need for loves young dream
mummy I shall never be to you or others of your ilk

So on that cold November day
when you came into this world so full of life
tears of joy I could not fathom,
choked instead within my constricted throat
the hate for your daddy burning in my belly
where should have been the child,
my own love spun in reams of gold.
Instead you are held in mothers arm
family cooing warmly at the bedside of prosperity.

and I the wicked spinster am alone
struck from the picture for my simple lies,
the simple truth that spilled out as blood
the day the virgin became a woman.
Too soon to know that women are sooner made
as mothers are forgotten in passions flare,
I declare my jealousy rages
not for a brothers love or child
but for bitterness that his raping seed denied me.

Wednesday's child

this is my day -
spent heavy in tears,
where mingles blood
from broken veins
that cry in painful meaning,

were you to stoop low -
to meet my lowered gaze,
what words would form
upon your curling lips,
are there any more
I love you's?

did this denial
beat raging against you heart;
in the clam of night
when you laid
above my quaking form,

they spoke solemnly,
of splintered girls and whole men,
who woke to desire
throbbing fast below waves
of knowing better,

your cold hands searched
so effortless;
for the fruits of labours,
caught my breath
and stole it for your own,

this dream keeps me;
worn and waking
from life's new dawn,
I wait lonely now
in the half light of your shadow.

laggard

Behind me you hang -
head low
arms limp
feet dragging in the dirt.
Skirt tattered and filthy;
skillfully you cry.

Why can't you move faster
instead you are slowing me down.
Round winding corners
I hoped to lose you;
confuse you with my
change of directions.

How you scream,
when I dream I am free -
seeing my destination
coming into focus
in the distance;
yet your resistance binds me.

If I could hate you child,
wild and unruly -
truly I could leave
but you breathe the same breath.
So unless I am dead
in my head you shall always be there.

I am a Death watch song

I am a death watch song;
lack luster firefly
languishing in dark
cavernous rooms.
Beyond night waits life
confined to longing,
heart beaten helix
turning on a moonbeam.

Fractious with envy
as the aurora beckons,
her name slips
from parched tongue
full and fat.
Fated to lay still
stoned in silence;
crimson after-burn.

Blacken eye.
Ashen skinned
fingers curl
towards a burning sun.
Skinned to bone
alabaster bleach;
reaching a precipice
of released denial.

paper mâché darling

I am not your play pretend rag doll;
puppet girl on pieces of string,
bringing you back to where you left off
with your pretty wife.

I had a life before you;
yet you wish me to forget
melt into an idol of domestic design.
How I resigned myself to loving your vision.

A prison of desire wrapped up pretty in a red dress,
less if your way swayed me to naked distraction,
only a fraction of myself remaining.

an ugly night in Soho

I hadn't planned to make you smile
while laid flat on my back
legs spread at strange obtuse angles.
But that's what happens after a bottle of whiskey
and that was just mine.

Who cares about coke (diet please)
I'm a hard girl, a bad girl
who can handle her drink.
At least that was the thought
before you slapped me hard across the face.

Maybe it was when I spat in your face,
called you a bastard for doing it
with the girl at the bar;
flirting over her low cut top,
cleavage spilling into my JD.

Such a charmer with your words and looks.
All coy when you catch my eye
but I spy you getting all excited;
passing glances over the exchange of money.
Were paying for drinks or something more?

She's bound to be a whore,
you expect it out in Soho.

They come (or cum) like buses three at a time.
Well, you were supposed to be mine
or you were before we got here.

I sat in the gutter to think streaks
of best placed liquid liner running
over a red cheek and fattening lip.
I'd say you hit like a girl
only you'd come back for more.

I don't think I'm a jealous type
that hypes up over some slut dressed in red,
but you feel you way through the dark clubs
as though have a radar attached to your cock,
a ticking clock wheedling them out.

So I sit and you stand
all grand in your own defense
as I look around lost, feeling foolish and small.
Not the tall five foot eight blonde that you love
but a drunken tart with too much cleavage
and a skin full of drink.

If I blink you will be gone?

I've done it again and again,
will you refrain from leaving me here,
make it clear nothing has changed
or slink of with her, the looker
into the night.

the game

Stack them high,
sell yourself cheap
or keep silent
in the background
of a darkened alley.

I have a line
that runs
right round the block,
into the good part
of a bad town.

Bowler hats and brollies
reading papers;
a crumpled financial times
to hide the burning
that waits below the waist.

I forgot that you
and the others
walked on past there
on your way to the pub;
a cup match playing
on a widescreen TV.

So when you looked
across your shoulder
and mouthed to our friends,
"There's that whore",
you stopped half way
when you caught my face

buried in the waist
of some unknown stray.
My waiflike figure
bobbing for a penny
or a pound.

There was no sound
just silence that echoed
of piss stained walls.
And I, full of them,
cannot call your name.

Home is not home anymore;
just a door that I pass
on my way to places,
faces that I
will never know.

I don't show up for the match
but catch something funny;
spend days
cramping and crawling on the floor.

I don't love you anymore.

I never loved you,
not even
at the start.

the dark water nymph

Exhaustion whips deathly a fragile beast,
with splintered bone limbs wrapped bloody in gauze.
Malevolence's cause hangs limp mid air,
eastern winds free, un-tethered from their cause.

Black eyed crows sit perched on twisted braches,
staring intently waiting to swoop low;
on lies that trickle from oil slick feathers,
festering skeletal remains that flow.

Red river curving, ragged over rocks,
flesh grazing over drowning sediment.
Phantom fading; lost dreams bound in white lace,
a watery grave for loves sentiment.

He shot her dead, a name they never knew,
for on that day, his love for her was true.

the God squad

my born again friends have gone;
relinquished into the light of better days
where they sop up the meaning of tears
falling from the eyes of angels,
singing with luminescent voices
the praises of a Lord and master they cannot fathom.

clapping hands and merriment permeates their souls;
speaking with twisted inflection and meaning,
spirits inflicting some form of happiness of another
until they are weary of the substance;
full to bursting with good intent and intentions.

they walk dark streets in the middle of the night
searching corners for homeless men,
who cling tight to meth and used cigarette butts,
wrapping them in coarse blankets
before putting them in the back of their suburban family cars,

driving through a moral fog that clouds the road
back to their place of worship;
where they wash their stinking bodies of filth and sin -
suit them, guide them in the righteous path
towards the electric light of social sanctity,

when the devil raises his glass they shy
from the burning insignia of the faithless,
unable to contextualise answers that fall short
in the mornings dawn of a new day,
fresh endeavours of the lowly stack high against the concrete city,

so they retire worn from efforts of salvation,
their own souls tainted with the glow of deeds;
to deep and dark to count until they fall
back onto resting laurels of fresh greenery,
the Christian stance of watching, judging but doing nothing.

night watch Death song

You whole

or broken husk.

Discarded
in earth
buried by two -

firm hands
blistered;
caught in fire grates.

Malice
a burning flame;

cylindrical melody
curves
indifferences sweet breath.

Hollow

ex
    hal
        a
           tio
              ns.

Until empty
loves sigh
rains

d
o
w
n

dampening spirits
black
charred remains.

Chalk bone stalks
stake graves
upon hallowed ground.

quiet house

Dip low between folds of cold white flesh
meshed together with twine.
Wine red groves bite deep;
skin bleeds and burns blue
before you rest your weary head
in my open palm.

Purple horizon gleams bitterly
the magenta flush of passion
lackluster when mustering the rush.
Your old fashioned desire stifled;
stiff with your thick fist
bruising across this chest.

How I reveled in your pedagogy state;
inflated ego weights down these days.
How I resent the deeper wounds
inflicted beneath the thin veil
of solicited untruths -
how malleable my supple form

Born of your blood and bone
skin sown with golden threads
picked and pulled to persuasion.
I am your temptation calling
gnawing sickly at your feet
reaching deaths oblivion in anti climax.

The Effigy of Self and Survival

Phoenix sunrise

From the dark corners
they enter.

Rooms which are
voids,
masks of meaning,
shadows that linger
in my heart.

Breaking away
from the gloom;
to bask warm in the morning.
Better images of themselves,
catching fires
in the breath
of angels.

When I come
in the morning
watching the firelight grow;
knowing with mourning
deception is the
only reason,

I cry aloud.

High above the dim voice
sings a halo of pity,
caught in the rays
of a blooming sun.
Here she sits
rocking and
screaming,

This is what they made me.

How can I teach her?

Reach out my hands
and capture her sorrow.
Does this despair
know no ending?
Sending her slowly
to madness.

Come little child
I love you.

Forgive me these silent years.

Forgotten, you laid restless
until no more
could be taken.
From you I stole
your voice
so high and angelic.

On my knee I beg you

for simple words
of affections.
I wrap these
around you;
a simple blanket of
honesty.

I was as lonely as you.

Broken pieces
scattered to the winds.
So hold tight
dear one,
for no longer shall you
wait impatient in the dark.

Into the dark they are receding.
Into the black I shall send them.

We are the truth
and they are the lie.
To die now would serve us
no purpose.

Into the light I raise you.

The effigy of self
and survival,
too long I have let them
take you.

No more.

For we are calling,
calling my baby,
my self,
and we are holding.

Together in blood.

Together.

We are grown.

girl loves girl loves girl

undertones of flesh
catch hot beneath these sheets
of love, that bow and rise
to the melody of our hearts,
capture my breath;
I am restless in my longing -
a lusting for your lips,

curling hips that lift or drift
towards the unfurling petals
of your sweet umber,
to slumber I - in waves
of coiling ecstasy.
Humming bird - I quiver
at your touch,

to linger in the furrows
of fields of skin,
that spread content
across this white expanse,
to sleep my love -
to dream
of waking in dawns cool morning
and begin again anew,
this simple love
burning with passionate hunger.

secret love notes

Thoughts stagnate
into grooves, a

delicious delirium

where
I am
confounded in
my dreaming
of you;

only you;

knowing that I,
hours
from your touch.

Breathe.

On my cheek;
how weak my heart
when pulled
far from your reach.

Give me darkness -
I
long
for salvation,
sick notes
of heart songs
are falling on deaf ears.

You are not near.
My voice
cannot carry
'cross fields
to where you rest.

Bring me back
whole
again,
to where knowing
your skin
warms these cool bones.

And when returned
into the sanctum
of your heart
I shall

sigh

in fullness of my being;

for only this
is living.
None can deny,
separation causes
my heart to bleed.

Dear,
sweet love;
love me
and if loving likes,
then liking becomes

love

and
I
am home.

a love so strong

endless days carried
the tears of trepidation -
across the divides
of oceans and great lands -
parting their earthly form
from one another's reach -
unspeakable desire
coursing in heat waves
across the plains,

a secret love:
that unspoken
never passed the cracked lips
of parched words -
wooden stakes the charge
of the heretic woman -
delighted by the form
of breast beneath a veil

woven dreams scattered
in dust storms -
ripping the remains
of dead angels
from the ground
where they fell
from heavens grasp -
released to man's
restless hunger

passing days
stretching long -
into horizon's eye
could not abate
the taciturn leanings -
inspired prayers
capturing lust
in delicate hands

when night enveloped
the desert sky:
stars sinew pinpricks
of streaking light
these two forms -
woman -
crept across the ocean's
riding waves
of deepest blues -
cresting on horses' backs

beneath the open air
these two:
merged into realms
beyond the sparks
of night -
combining partials
to form one
beyond heaven's wake

a love so strong
it would tear their hearts
to speak
the name of
beckoning faith -
as earth's reach
opened up
to hold them close -
within her convex
heart.

falseness of truth

truth is:
the girl with
no name -
walking through fields
of moulding harvest -
gone to seed

truth is:
years
crushed beneath lies -
rasping for breath -
waiting for
the right words

truth is:
false unless -
spoken in tongues
against the cross
of saviour's
broken remains

truth is:
a fateful need
laid bare -
in the sarcophagus
of child's
scorpion spite

truth is:
lost in dust
passed over -
form lost
beneath the deaf -
deception
of lies

moon

she is my moon:
full of glory
in her orbital state
a perpetual movement
between the divide
heaven's guide

I bath naked in her light
as darkness envelopes
the souls hunger,
she leads me
leashed towards
states of passion

swathed in supple lips
that press firm
against my mouth,
full of her
full of night's embrace
beneath sheets of white

the waking dawn
calls her
from my arms,
lifting her back
to positions above me,
I falter to a static lingering

my eyes raised
searching the skies
broad horizon
until day's light
fades to dark
and I may begin again

the feminine violation

Feminine divine light;
lost beneath soot filled lungs -
burnt out ashen women
staring through broken eyes
as they die inside.
Washing up dishes -
choking on white bile;
swallowing down servility.

Pinned specimens
on floral patterned sheets -
speculum filled wombs
entombed in fertile deliverance.
Wrap them in swaddling
suffocate the screaming -
feed consumptive mouths
clamped tight round brown wounds.

Our homologous state
binding the feral men
to ways and means
of acceptable behaviour.
How they measure themselves
by our bold beauty.
only to leave us wasted -
empty husks of ourselves.

letter 2003

Yesterday I read a report
from two thousand and three;
about me and my
condition.

A brief history taken
by a man in a suit,
who tutted and nodded
in agreement
or not
at the statements I made.

Always explaining myself.

He had no idea;
no compulsion to understand
that I knew
what I was doing.

Listed out
point after point
my complaints,
my symptoms,
where I scored on the scale.

How I failed to accept
his extended offer of a
cure.
No more lying and crying,
no more starving
until there is nothing left.

A note of my rebuff;
my disinclination to follow
his prescribed program.

I knew it wasn't me.

The final satanic verse
in bold black print;
BMI: 16.6
Diagnose: Anorexia

How these words mock me now;
kneeling on the floor
as I sift through paper
ready for recycling.

My life waiting to be made
into something more useful;
shiny and new,
its past life forgotten.

I hold this letter in my hand,
tearful;
sad for what I was,
what I have become;

Normal.

Cured my own
careful rebuilding of myself.

Folding it back into the envelope
I place it in the "to keep" pile
and while I carry on
my heart skips too many beats.

For I mourn you, girl
that lived back then,
and I welcome this woman
who has grown from her pain.

I am shamed by wanting to return;
damned by life never to again.
I cry for all I lost
when I starved you out.

Forgot that when I did so
I was starving myself out too.

for you

There are days when love
runs thick and smooth
through veins;
courses towards an open heart.

And yet;

there are moments when your heart
for all its love
must turn upon the world;
shut itself in a darkened room.

When I see you sleeping;
watch the rise and fall
of your chest,
I rest knowing that sleep
may bring you some ease
or relief from the long day.

And here in the dark corners
of a room we call our own

I wait.

Patient.

Holding in my hand
all of myself for you,
gripping tight the knowing
that all things change
and pass into blurred memories.

So when you wake
from your slumber,
to be greeted with a sweet kiss
from these patient lips,
you will know;

between light and dark
within the shadows gaze
am I.
Your love and lover;
ready to open myself to you
as is a flower
waiting for the sun
in a new dawn.

And I shall give
you everything,
for everything to me
is you.

if I could be

Dear Fee,
you come to me
with tiny hands
calling my name -
" 'am...'am"
you say,
your little mouth
cannot make its way
around the S,

you pull at my fingers;
desperate to show
your baby doll
decked out in her finery -
jacket inside out
she has no pants on,
but your pride
shines through
your gapped tooth smile,

your mummy
doesn't want you anymore;
so you
have been deposited
into the hearts
of others -
whose own home
has become
your place of safety,
when I visit them
I secretly come
to visit you,

I want to be your mummy;
to teach you
how to count to ten
and spell your name
in little letters -

I want to tuck
your tiny body
under the covers a night,

it will be me;
who runs to your cries
when you wake
in the dark of the night -
nightmares dancing
underneath your eyes,
me who whispers
sweet words of comfort
as you fall back
to dreamless sleep,

it should be me;
dressing you
for the first day at school -
standing at the front gates
beaming nervously
as you run
towards your friends -
towards happy days,

dear fee,
I wish you knew
that I love you,
so much of me
I see in you -
I wish you knew
you have a home
in my heart -
that I would be mummy
even just for one day

for my Mother and the fourth star

reflective distortion

I

As I slept late into the day,
sunlight streaming through windows,
you crept out of bed and hid
in the un-swept corner of the room,
buried yourself in cracks;
broken floor boards I had not repaired,
I had not cared to mind them
for I had you upon which to look.

How I took your beauty for granted
as it laid flush against my chest,
resting as my breath played in your hair.
If I stared too long my eyes filled with tears,
joy streaming across cheeks of pale ivory;
How I should have placed
one diamond upon your finger

I linger now in the dark,
lamps off, television turned down low.
How slowly time passes as I search
deep into my heart chambers
for grief's rusted nail embedded deep;
so I may bleed gradually to my death upon our bed,
where we read love poems to one another.

When I discover something dusty,
musty paper pushed between two boards,
my aching heart wastes away in desire.
Unfurling creased pages to see your words
skating in blue ink across to two sheets,
greeting me with visions of your violet eyes.

I hold you close towards my mouth
to kiss you full upon the lips;
slipping back to griefs dreamlike lie,

dying in your arms again
and gone.

Turned to ash and bone,
thrown towards the open window to drift
away towards the morning breaking.
You wrapped around my middle
singing love songs and drinking wine,
time forgotten
regret unknown.

II

Regret unknown;
sown deep before the breath of day
exhales from pursed lips
drawn tight in ignorant slumber.
How my arrogance of desire
has tarnished your sweet embrace
pulling from my outstretched arms
into those of another.

Blackness shrouds you,
swirling over your blonde head;
you are dead, wrapped in lace and cotton
forgetting us, how we talked.
If I meet you half way, will you sway
back to where I stand open hearted
full of sorrow for misplacing love;
a dove resting silent in my palm.

Fear expands with your chest,
blood rushing to limbs seeking air.
How I care for you when you are crippled,
a ripple of tears swimming in your eye.
Should I have fought to clear your lungs,
drained out water seeping into the lining
of your withered spirit lost at sea;
yet consumed by me, I cannot see you drifting.

Lifting out of a frozen ocean's ripping tide
to ride above, over head with reddened lips.
Slipping from this life to another,
I am rudderless;
lost in seas of endless dreams unraveling.
No rope to bind myself to masts or mountains,
counting days until life may slip from fingers,
as you slipped from my grasp when you needed it most.

III

Just before dawn I wake
from a shiftless dream state.
Limbs tangled in rags of sheets
tears lingering on eye lids
burning red raw from grief weight.
A state of angered longing
burning steady in a broken heart.

If I start to turn, I am fearful
that your side will remain empty;
cold from your lack of presence;
a resonance of my stupidity freezing me
out of a life that I claimed as my own.
For I had grown weary of believing
that tomorrow would always be
a better day than this.

Now I miss your warmth caught in blankets,
head rested heavy on your feather pillow.
My courage has deserted me;
freed itself to wander lonesome in the night,
frightening small children who remain
lost within the trappings of a nightmare.
Staring vacant as I lose myself
in memories of you over me.

Yet I see you breathing deeply on my left -
curled up tight against the winter cold,
bold as is belonging here, you shall always remain.
I refrain from reaching out
touching the bare skin dimmed in first light,
slight, your tiny frame sleeping.
How did you come back to me
when I fled far from here and you?

This aching head and heart does not dare
to care beyond the knowing,
reasons shift and change with the turning day.
If I stay still, you shall stay
and I pray you do not wake.
Remembering pains me to a slow death,
breathless for joy is springing
singing low and deep in my soul.

For I am whole with regret and knowing,
showing all I am to you;
new love has blossomed from something dusty,
the rusty shards worn smooth.
Grooves in which you hid give way,
opening places for us to lay;
stay wound in one another's soul,
bold am I for this love is renewed.

when I lay down in your bed of ashes

Flashes of us out in the sun
naked on the grass as time
passed us by uncaring.
Staring intently into eyes of a lover
another soul merged into my own.

How we danced to the tune of our hearts,
burning desire firing synapses
until exhausted we laid still;
just to hear each other breathing,
reeling from sensations of lust
pounding in our chests.

Practice, we said,
laughing at ourselves dreaming,
beaming until three babies came crying,
laughing out of our love.

Wrapped in arms and hearts
how passion shifts and lifts.

How fast they grow.
How slow I was to see that you
stood stooping, eyes seeming tired.
But so many mouths to feed and laces to tie.
I cried for you, for them, when you said
you would be dead in a year.

And now you have gone

far from them and me.
I see your face so often in the stars
when stroking the scar left on my heart.
The start of grief seems never to end
but sends me reeling from myself.

When I lie down in your bed of ashes
deep in the night the fright of longing

moves me to death's own door.
No more do I breathe with joy,
but toy with the thought of leaving them here
so I may be nearer to you.

Would you forgive me with faith
if I walked to your place of hiding
with grace and opened arms?
Your charms are too strong and I long
to know the feeling of being again.

When I lie down in your bed of ashes,
I mourn for myself.
Selfish is loss,
for losing you was losing me
and all the space that was between.

horripilation

Under sheet of red velvet
run long stemmed fingers.

Come.

Sigh.

Breathe.

May I meet you half way;
between dusk and dark
to embark upon journeys
to valleys deep and wide.

Such roads spread far
beyond the reach of moral men -
gallant knights have rested
wretched at the wayside;
forgotten dreams lingering on their lips.

These hips turning
urging on the reaches of your touch.
Tender words that brush
smooth against my cheek.

How I seek you out.

All shallow doubt drifts;
melodious moments of heart beats.

Solidarity stands against no woman.

I am your voice
as you are mine.
Between time
we greet with kisses,
full and red,
cradle places of wondered lust;

thrust forward with hunger
until I slumber in the crook
of your muscled arm.

Charming you;
watching my eyes
flutter closed to dreamscapes.

Holding hair and tears in your hands,
deep days and long nights
under starlight burning day back.

Fearful of the dawn,
graceless I gather you;
in hands and mouths and meaning
seemingly seeing eternal
the youth of love
in its age old ageless entirety.

woman of shadows

I just want to be a woman;
fully fledged and pledged
to no man and all;
a school of thought
that grows with the shape
and making of a mind.

No heart can contain
the sing song melodies
of evolution.

This miracle mars me to disbelief.

Thieves of the night
fought hard,
over small dips
and grooves
to prove their worth
as men.

I am slight;
a frightful contradiction
that runs fearful
towards the light
and back into the shadows.

Oh the burn.

Sun's strong glow
on white curdled flesh
that meshes together the way
forward and back.

I crack under the weight of being.

Seeing all this
I reach
towards your open hand,
to curl tender
in your outstretched palm.

Hold me.

Wrap me in words and lips;
an embrace of knowing love
fits like a glove.
You over me,
me inside all of you.

So true the way I walk;
stalk about the wayside
until full light
and day illuminates the shade.

I am the shadow walker;

into this new day I glide,
full of flesh and bone
so home to you,
begging for love and lust.

A simple touch and I am yours.

A word of truth and then;
all woman

I am bare before you.

down by the water

Remember the aftertaste?

A bitter reverb of your being
that runs rings around my heart,
until its final beat
jumps out of time.

I am mine;

regaining that pace of life
where being a wife
and mother
to you,
a lover unwanted
means I am not dead,
but moving
between the shadows of day.

So they say this is
recovery.

A lie that lingers
with a sharp bite.
I wish I could spite myself
into being a more
positive
woman.

Yet laying here staring
at the stars,
a strangers breath
the only comforting warmth
from a cold night working,
skirting along the banks
of the river.

I can swim.

How I wish it wasn't so.
So slow I could dip
deep into the cool pools
of muddy blood.
A stagnant stench of flesh
creeps fast into my veins.

Slip low under the veil of night.

So in spite of this,
I am all things
and nothing
wrapped into one.
I could whisper into the black
as I go slack with release
"I won"
and I am gone far
from here
and us.

foreign friend

She is all things.

I
the insufferable jester
walk behind in shadows.
Watching a smile
dance across her face.

There are words;

countless
yet few and far between.

I lean closer
so I may drink them in
and know
I am known.

Where have you been
sweet friend?
Not fiend
that watches my face
to see my mourning.

May I smile
while you watch me,
teach me ways
and means to be.

And what of these
or where they go,
or rises to from here.

No fear exists.
Can I be
in return all things?
In kind
remind her of beauty

that runs silent
in the dark.

This heart
is breaking;
for the joy is singing
as she walks
through the park,
humming our tune.

for MaC

there is nothing better than sex in the kitchen

There is nothing
better than sex in the kitchen;
with you laid out flat
like a fat cat that's got the cream.
How I dream of that grin
spread as far and wide as my thirty-two and a half inch legs
wrapped around your chest.

When we rest we smoke;
not in bed but wrapped in sheets
and shirts in the garden.
Huddled together for extra warmth
and the heat that greets me
rising from your body;
as an invisible steam
moves me back to places we have just been.

Blowing smoke rings in your face
you race to cup your hands around mine;
so bone fine and pale white.
Light from the window
making long shadows across dewy grass,
until at last you reach
underneath my layers of wrapping.

And so strapping are you;
when you run those working hands
all over my convex curves.
I swerve into your arms
falling fast into the deep pools
of love that turn towards the sun.

I am undone by your lust

So we lay in the flower beds
full of geraniums and daisies;

crazy with a passion that lifts
and dips as the tides of time.
I am mine and yours
gorged in greedy hunger and need;
freed from all that
which lingered before.

ashes to ashes

your panacea has remedied nothing:
I am still mourning you -
walking silent through our house
shrouded in black lace and lavender,
damp eyes passing over surfaces
dusty since your last touch.

promises that echo from these walls
taunt me with a mocking tone,
sweet calls of I love you -
a slap across the face
smiling in the wake
of my many well tended tears.

did your belief transport you
from the confines of our marital bed,
where your rotting corpse
twisted from consciousness to indifference,
to a place above me or below -
no matter, for I cannot reach you.

when the many grief stricken friends
returned to their homes -
grateful to leave the stench of death
that will not remove itself from here,
they held one another tight
in warm loving arms full of life.

as I sat at our kitchen table,
folding your napkin no longer used -
the effort of breathing
overwhelmed my heart,
its broken pieces scattered
across our 1972 lino flooring,
six days gone and no words
no moaning wail has passed my lips,
the phone has stopped ringing
the television mute,

soap operas played out in silent mocking
images that mean little to me.

perhaps death eases with time -
years of weeping turning my flesh
to dried parchment,
until I falter and turn with your ashes
into the wind as it runs through the garden -
and we merge into an eternal dust.

if the wings of Icarus had been made of steel

Night's deep ebony encloses with stealth the coy heart.

In visions young men do dream of birds' wings;
strapped to backs of boys to lift them
high above the open fields and rivers running to the sea,
where toiling men sweat until brittle boned they crumble
to dust and so become the land that broke them.

Chained to days of toil in the beating rays,
they gaze beyond crackled breaths to rest
a weary eye of skies of ocean blue.
The concave atrium of a broken heart looms unholy,
for no woman can suppress a need for freedom;
no curling hips or lips to burn out lust beyond flesh.

Old women weep at the foot of an open grave
where enslaved sons have run from wakefulness;
fallen for forgotten dreams where un-woken they are full.
If the Wings of Icarus had been made of steel,
men would not weep in skin and bone,
but craft great delights of fancy

to lift them up and carry them home.

Death turns clever in my mind

Death turns
clever in my mind.
Your sepulcher
structured to contain
faithless remains;
framed in lace.

Slip slick from hands
washed in holy
water.
Blessed by men
in robes of rich
purple;

colours of passion
burning in loins
of swathed flesh;
pressed firm
towards the divine
crucifix.

You are my
Stigmata.
Bleeding wounds
un-heeling
reeling towards sacred
words.

Run from lips
stitched with twine.
Sacramental
wine sipped slow;
until drunken
I ferment in grief.

re crim in ation

Under

weeping willow

hangs death.

Two foot rope

swinging
in
the wind.

How I stand
to the right of you
frightened of you

in all your glory.

Sinews   str   etc   hed

Dead eye hanging
On a loose lip

    S
   l
  i
 p
   p
    i
     n
      g

from cracked skull

                        shining bone
catching   moonlight.

                    Stars
                    bright
                    burning

                Angels F U R Y
                    <u>scorched</u>

        upon   frosted ground

                    soundless

        re   crim   in   ation

otiose

If life consists of waiting
patient for the day,
when undone the weary
and the meek
shall meet their maker;

the fiery voice of redemption
shall turn to ash
all that walk this day;
for idle is the heart

Unloved.

Unknown.

Undone.

We are all such sinners;
liars of a faith
that hold rules and reams
of parchment to our lives
until we are broken.

On bended knee
with clasped hanging;
begging for a savior
to offer a pittance
of forgiveness.

Mutter your Hail Mary's
and douse you head
with holy water.

For the slaughter of the young
shall continue
into the long
endless
night.

incandescence

The coil of love;
internal
in the canvas of my breast,
where red meets
your lips.
Grazes the tender tips
of all of me.

And I see in you;
words that form
around kisses.
Lifting dark skies
above the din.

Until entwined
the all of this woman;
flesh and bone
lays open before the dawn.
And you
the warming sun

Move me to life.

to an end

Sheathed in gold
stands delinquent
a child of bold design.
Resigned to sit
static in the afterglow
of a burning sun.

Blind eyes see;
drawing a flex from dark,
where glides the hands
of marksmen
trained upon the unseen flesh.

Regress.

In turn
a screaming man of grief's
own making,
lays wrecked upon a shore
of rock and bone
stoned to silence.

Divine.

Oh divine light
relinquish these sins;
for lips have parted
to breath an utterance
of forgiveness.

So undone
to the tides of change.
We begin again
and so end another day.

Pulling Wings from Dragonflies

the fingersmith

You finger-paint in menstrual blood
as I wither from your bitterness -
turned, for my nakedness disturbs you.

Chilled heart spilling your venomous, poisoned
chalice. How I cup you in my womb
too soon filled with septic fever.

I cradled you as I-child
nestled between pubis and sternum

filling up
and up
and up

until I am swollen.

Vertical symmetry as we collide,
consigned to replay memories.

With needle and thread I stitch
internal wounds stemming the effusion
as you rush from me.

Unclean fluids of tear stained regret
for I forget you are trespassing here,
mortal flesh meshed to your limb.

I am slim, thin to snapping,
brittle from over use,
affuse, you cleanse me.

Continuously drowning -
lungs filled, for I am under
as I have always been.

The final silent image of you smiling,
you know I am undone.

genetic disorder

Naked
sprawled in pale moonlight -
awoken by your desire.

Burning instincts
lay illicit in my womb -

fractious heart beats;
drum
to
your
rhythmic
breath.

Metronomic
calm that soothes
beneath my sternum.

Sliced open to cold air
with bone handle knives
fashioned under hailstorm skies;
sinews dulled somber as death.

Engulfed in flesh,
your afterbirth staked to earth
reverberates a wet lung cry -
dried husks spread upon the ground.

I have carved out space for you,
speculum clasped in withered hand.
Skin resistant to my digging,
an infringing

Push   Pull

Umbilicus intrusion
sits contrite within my belly,
bile filled discontent.

A reflux,
acidic bite
after burn on a thinning tongue,
you are my myzocytosis.

embryonic ghost

She is the all things
and none.
Cloned of bone chine shards -
fractious design of delinquent hands.
Stands solicitous in dark
reflections of an anguished state.

Gilded from flesh
blood rich embers spiraling
towards open skies.
Bitter night air biting at breasts
weary for elusive restful slumber.

Skewed reflex ,
a reflux vibration
coils in my belly.
Swollen.
Your seed does linger,
infringing on my being,
suckling substance from thinning womb.

Mercury breath
snatches beauty lost
behind clouded eye glass specters.

Our baby cries hungry
for I have forgotten where she lays.

Strayed in utero caverns
to beseech the waning glory of delusion.
I am barren, for broken I have bled,
fed you until full your greed unabated
consumes my flesh for famine.

blind death

Chromatic dream;
spleen filled bile
silos into acid veins.
Your shunt stemming
slow flowing grief -
scattered shattered tear drops
cyclops woman.

Myopic eye
captures
retina burn
in an reflective helix.
Coiled breath
resplendent in your belly
a concave enclave.

Fastidious - your jealousy
unabated glory
tickles your under tongue.
Thick white lies
lapping at your mouth -
obtuse angles
rapturous in serendipity.

Refracted, we are
gallant heroes
of whispered sibilant
dreams.
Screaming on the breath
of furrowed grave -
opened bare
to midnight cold wind.

sexual disqualification

You are mystic,
metallic claw hooked in eyelids
between heaven.
You are urethral benedictine
serpent headed quarry,

waxen skinned under belly
steel sting stitching -
itching between your open
sore soaked embrace -
flesh connected endosteum .

I am filament:
flinted chipped to shards -
a void reflecting time
space enveloping breath.

You are my asphyxia.

Deep water blackout
free dive
radiation burn
strips skin.
I am estrogen pure.

Powder white ash.

Transgender genealogy
counter parts fused,
Desire: Oedipus Complex
how your dream
sex.

Sexual dimorphism.

Your stiff fingered talon
tickles undersides,

tantalising spell bound
your hallucinogen dreamscape,
I am mystic.

how long must this last

How long must this last -
the fast backward interplay
of your tongue in my cheek
and I, meek and dainty,
flush red.
I am gasping as you kiss;
caress each tiny line
that has spread across my face
with a pace I cannot conceal.

How you feel beneath your shirt
as I skirt for your skin.
I am sin - sinning - sinner
with fingers poised to perfect
the timely excitement that runs hot -
soft and solid from your being
seeing you are naked, I am nude.

I am tantalised, energised
ready to run smooth against your flesh -
meshed to your body
as if I were you epithelial covering.
Smothering you with a lust
old and rust - dusted off for you.
Too soon it shall end and my death
will abate your dream;
seamless I shall flow from your arms.

How you'll charm me with tears
fears of loneliness lost -
tossed aside as we bid farewell
through river beds of Hades.

Wading as far as you dare
before currents lift your feet
as wash you away with me.

How long must this last
past the night into day;
for I sway with my love lust need.\,
but must concede to breathe
one last breath
for you to inhale
and wail with grief.

my virtuoso villain

Virtuoso villain,
taken of your pound of flesh,
stretched across a green felt board
hoarded into heaps of forgotten trophies.
Once I was your prize possession -
you should have burnt me at the stake.

Pulling wings from dragonflies.

Pinned limbs stretched - straining
gaining no relief from mumbled psalms -
palms up turned searching for recrimination.
Where are these Gods that spoke to me
drifted from my dream in clouds of fury;
gory remains lay stark in stillness.

You, my languishing dick-tator,
hater of female sex organism -
orgasm that sprung from lips

blossoming.

Benign contortions mixing with your fluid
gestures sequestered on fat tongue.

Your muffled breath floats -
sins are solidified as your rigor mortis limbs
becomes flaccid in the gaseous streams.
I am dreamlike fear captured in your eye
sliced in two by your giant ego.

I flounder in your fluid
gush
rush of ecstatic desire.
Rubbed red raw
embedded
through nights long lie.

Harboring your misfit intentions
inventions of a mind misplaced.

I am voodoo doll pin pricks
staked to your glory.

electra

Do not include me
in your wayward fondling.
I was rampant beneath these sheets
before
your hands shifted towards my warmth.
Swarming about a fragile frame -
blame riddled bone shafts
hollowed out until concave -
overworked.

I am Electra.

I dance naked underneath the moon
cold - blue skinned.
Slimmed to starved I am consuming
self centered cells -
melded maligned to divinity.
Your overwhelming urge to claim
girls as your own blood
floods my mouth

I am drowning.

Let me lay silent in your arms
as you pander the ample curve
of flesh.
Beneath shallow breath I am leaving.
Free, I shall slip from your embrace,
with grace I shall leave.

I am your biology.

Bound with fists and flushed passion
fashioned from Freud's own text,
Watch me I am burning -
ash lifting into blood red skies,
I am spread sprawling bawling
spawning a multitude stillborn lies.

I am my own complex.

I am Electra.

circumlocution

You use too many words when we walk;
talking about nothing that matters
avoiding all the things that should be said
instead you rant about day.

The this and that,
the girls in the office that annoy your moral
sensibilities.

They slide out of your mouth
so fast I struggle to catch the syllables
that roll into one another and they dribble
from your tongue caught between two fat lips.

Sometimes you slip up and I know
you are meaning something else;
that lingers below the surface
of a mundane everyday life.

Husband and wife bound by vows,
meaningless as the paper you lost
when you cleared out the draw
where I kept my precious things.

Junk.

Funky rubbish that I collected
you said;
it was getting in the way
making the place look untidy.

I wonder if you could lift me
would you throw me out too?

Threadbare feelings like my over worn shirt
that I iron myself.
You say you are not my slave,
I hadn't thought you were.

So we walk and you talk
and I listen to your chit chat;
drift of into the pitched hum of your nothing
to remember the day I last spoke
and meant it.

So far away
I think it was
or could have been

"I do."

of love I spoke

You don't speak to me
across the table.
You rest
two thin palms
inside one another.

I cannot recover
from your words.

Your lips purse
in thoughtful poise
so no further noise
may pass between them.

Or us?

The rush of love
has drawn back;
sweet nothings parched
and brittle
about the floor.

No more desire
to run ragged
across the stretch
of long winter nights.
The delight of you
no more a salvation
for me.

You are free.

So run
far from here and this;
my cure has drawn
no sanctity
from statements of obvious.

I came to you
divided and drawn;
blood that spilled
once thrilled
your sense of romance.
Now the mess of me
reminds you of my weakness;
subtle lines of poetry;
torn papers that litter
and spark distain.

All the tender remains;
tinder dry fire flies.

Let us burn our memories
and return to dust;
forget the words and tears.

My fears do not abate.

So run my love,
from yourself or me.
Come cleanly back
with open arms
when knowing is clear,

for I am here,
remaining tender
to the emptiness of black.

NeoPoiesis
a new way of making

in ancient Greece, poiesis referred to the process of making
creation – production – organization – formation – causation
a process that can be physical and spiritual
biological and intellectual
artistic and technological
material and teleological
efficient and formal
a means of modifying the environment
and a method of organizing the self
the making of art and music and poetry
the fashioning of memory and history and philosophy
the construction of perception and expression and reality

NeoPoiesis Press
reflecting the creative drive and spirit
of the new electronic media environment

www.ingramcontent.com/pod-product-compliance
Lightning Source LLC
Chambersburg PA
CBHW021013090426
42738CB00007B/774